READING POWER

Sports History

The Story of Baseball

Anastasia Suen

The Rosen Publishing Group's
PowerKids Press™
New York

Published in 2002 by The Rosen Publishing Group, Inc.
29 East 21st Street, New York, NY 10010

First Edition

Book Design: Michelle Innes

Suen, Anastasia.
The story of baseball / by Anastasia Suen.
    p. cm. — (Sports history)
Includes bibliographical references (p.) and index.
ISBN 0-8239-6000-5 (lib. bdg.)
1. Baseball—History—Juvenile literature. [1. Baseball—History.] I.
Title.
GV867.5 .S86 2001

                              2001001118

Manufactured in the United States of America

Contents

Beginnings

These boys are playing baseball. People have played stick-and-ball games like baseball for hundreds of years.

Baseball comes from a stick-and-ball game called rounders. Rounders was popular in the United States in the early 1800s.

By the 1830s, different forms of baseball were being played. In 1845, Alexander Cartwright and his team made a set of 20 rules for all teams to follow. Soon, people all over the United States began to play by these rules.

Alexander Cartwright started the Knickerbocker Base Ball Club, a team in New York City in 1845.

For many years, people believed that Abner Doubleday "invented" baseball in 1839. This is one of the oldest stories told about baseball. People who study baseball history now know that he did not invent baseball.

Abner Doubleday was a Union general in the Civil War.

By the late 1860s, people wanted to see and learn more about baseball. Many painters and photographers used baseball as a subject in their art.

IT'S A FACT!

Civil War soldiers spread the game of baseball to towns all over the northern and southern United States.

This is a painting of a baseball game from around the time of the Civil War.

The First Professional Team

The first professional baseball team was the Cincinnati Red Stockings. In their first season, they played about 56 games. There were only ten players on the team.

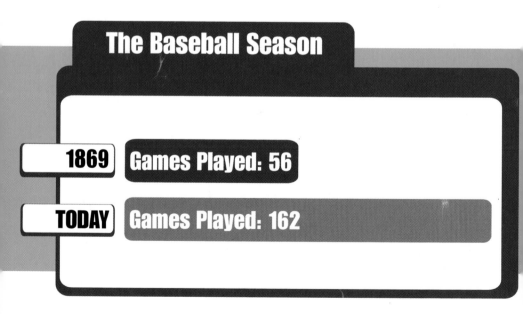

The Baseball Season

1869	**Games Played: 56**
TODAY	**Games Played: 162**

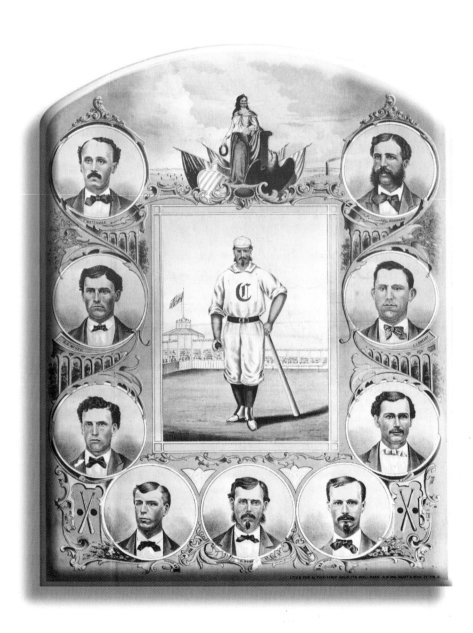

13

Leagues of Their Own

In 1876, the National League of Professional Base Ball Clubs started. In 1901, the American League started.

In 1903, the first World Series championship was played between the best teams from each league.

Thousands of people went to see the first World Series between the Boston Pilgrims and the Pittsburgh Pirates.

In 1943, the All-American Girls Professional Baseball League started. Professional women's baseball was very popular during the years of World War II. The league lasted until 1954.

Changes in Equipment

The equipment used by baseball players has changed over the years. Changes are made to the equipment to protect the players and to help them play better.

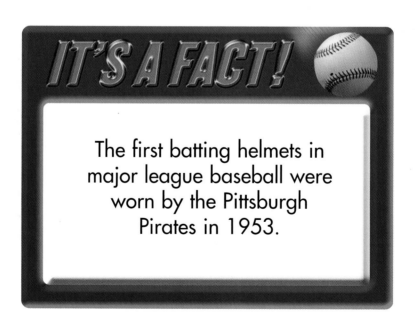

IT'S A FACT!

The first batting helmets in major league baseball were worn by the Pittsburgh Pirates in 1953.

Modern uniform

Helmet

Batting glove

Padding

19

Around the World

People all around the world love to play baseball and watch their favorite players. Many baseball players become heroes to their fans. Baseball is one of the United States' gifts to the world.

Baseball is very popular in Japan.

Babe Ruth

Roger Maris

Mark McGwire

Home Run Kings
Most Home Runs in a Single Season

1927	Babe Ruth	60 Home Runs
1961	Roger Maris	61 Home Runs
1998	Mark McGwire	70 Home Runs

Glossary

league (**leeg**) a group of teams that play
against each other in the same sport

professional (pruh-**fehsh**-uh-nuhl) an athlete who
gets paid to play a sport

rounders (**rown**-derz) a game played with a
ball and a bat in which players must run
around four bases to score points

World Series (**werld seer**-eez) a championship
played every year to see which is the best
baseball team

Resources

Books

Baseball
by James Kelley and James Buckley
Dorling Kindersley Publishing (2000)

Major League Baseball's Best Shots
by Johnny Bench
Dorling Kindersley Publishing (2000)

Web Site

Baseball Links
http://e-znet.com/kids/baseballlinks.html

Index

Word Count: 317

Note to Librarians, Teachers, and Parents

   If reading is a challenge, Reading Power is a solution! Reading Power is perfect for readers who want high-interest subject matter at an accessible reading level. These fact-filled, photo-illustrated books are designed for readers who want straightforward vocabulary, engaging topics, and a manageable reading experience. With clear picture/text correspondence, leveled Reading Power books put the reader in charge. Now readers have the power to get the information they want and the skills they need in a user-friendly format.